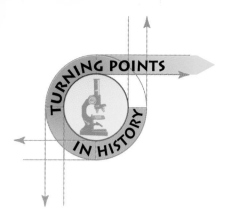

Penicillin

A Breakthrough in Medicine

RICHARD TAMES

LIBRARY

www.heinemann.co.uk
Visit our website to find out more information about **Heinemann Library** books.

To order:
☎ Phone 44 (0) 1865 888066
▤ Send a fax to 44 (0) 1865 314091
▭ Visit the Heinemann Bookshop at www.heinemann.co.uk to browse our catalogue and order online.

First published in Great Britain by Heinemann Library, Halley Court, Jordan Hill, Oxford OX2 8EJ, a division of Reed Educational and Professional Publishing Ltd. Heinemann is a registered trademark of Reed Educational & Professional Publishing Limited.

OXFORD MELBOURNE AUCKLAND JOHANNESBURG BLANTYRE
GABORONE IBADAN PORTSMOUTH NH (USA) CHICAGO

Designed by Robert Sydenham, Ambassador Design, Bristol
Originated by Ambassador Litho, Bristol
Printed in Hong Kong.

ISBN 0 431 06916 6
04 03 02 01 00
10 9 8 7 6 5 4 3 2 1

British Library Cataloguing in Publication Data
Tames, Richard, 1946–
Penicillin: a breakthrough in medicine. – (Turning points in history)
1. Penicillin – Juvenile literature
2. Penicillin – History – Juvenile literature
I. Title
615.3'295654

Acknowledgements
The Publishers would like to thank the following for permission to reproduce photographs:
Corbis: (Bettmann) pp. 4, 17, 20, 21, (Hulton Deutsch Collection) pp. 18, 19; Hulton Getty Images: pp. (John Chillingworth) 23, (Peter Pardy) 29; Mary Evans Picture Library: p. 6; MIG/Audio Visual Services/ICSM (St Mary's): pp. 12, 13, 14, 15, 22, 24; Science Photo Library: (Andrew McClenaghan) p. 26, (Marcello Brodsky) p. 28 (Sheila Terry) p. 27; Tames, Richard: pp. 5, 8, 11, 16, 25; Wellcome Institute Library, London: pp. 7, 9, 10.

Cover photograph reproduced with permission of Corbis.

Our thanks to Christopher Gibb for his help in the preparation of this book.

Every effort has been made to contact copyright holders of any material reproduced in this book. Any omissions will be rectified in subsequent printings if notice is given to the Publisher.

Contents

Some words are shown in bold, **like this**. You can find out what they mean by looking in the Glossary.

Hoping for a miracle

Race against death

In late summer 1943, 2-year-old Patricia Malone lay in New York's Lutheran Hospital with a rare form of blood **infection.** Doctors told her parents she would die within seven hours. Patricia's father had heard of a new wonder drug called penicillin, which was only being given to servicemen. He rang a journalist friend, begging him to help get some for Patricia.

The journalist rang the Surgeon General in Washington, DC. The Surgeon General rang Dr Chester Keefer in Boston. Keefer was in charge of the penicillin production project. He ordered a laboratory in New Brunswick, New Jersey, to make a supply of penicillin ready. Meanwhile Dr Collitti of the Lutheran Hospital set off to fetch it. With a police escort to clear the road, Collitti made it to New Brunswick and back within two hours. Collitti gave Patricia her first dose of penicillin with just ninety minutes to spare. Six weeks later Patricia had fully recovered and was home with her parents.

PENICILLIN SQUIBB
Sodium Salt of Penicillin
Contains 10,000 Florey units
No Preservative
KEEP BELOW 450 F.
Caution: New Drug--Limited
federal law to investigational use
E.R. Squibb & Sons, N.Y.
Biological Laboratories,
New Brunswick, N.J.

In 1943, 2-year-old Patricia Malone's life was saved when she was given the new wonder drug, penicillin.

A commemorative plaque at St Mary's Hospital, Paddington, London, records where Fleming discovered penicillin in 1928.

The first antibiotic

Patricia Malone was one of dozens of patients who were seemingly snatched from death as doctors explored just what penicillin could do. Discovered by accident by a British doctor, Alexander Fleming, in London in 1928, penicillin had remained a mystery for ten years. Then two Oxford researchers, an Australian, Howard Florey, and a German, Ernst Chain, struggled to develop penicillin into a usable drug.

They made their first trial on 12 February 1941, when they used it on Oxford policeman, Albert Alexander. He was dangerously ill with infections caused by a simple scratch from a rose bush, but within 24 hours his condition improved dramatically. Within a few days he was recovering strongly, but then their supply of penicillin ran out. The doctors desperately tried to recycle some of the drug from his urine. It was not enough, and Mr Alexander died of blood-poisoning on 15 March. This experience proved that curing with penicillin would be a matter of quantity as well as quality.

From magic to medicine

Western medicine began in ancient Greece. The roots of medicine in China and India are much older. All three systems had some ideas in common:

- that good health depended on keeping a balance of forces within the body
- that diet and climate affected health
- that many plants could heal illnesses.

Greek medical knowledge was summed up by Galen (about 129–216), whose books were still being used to train doctors in the 1600s.

Medieval doctors' treatments included drugs, bathing, bleeding and massage. They could fix simple **fractures** and **dislocations** and remove stones from the bladder and cataracts from the eye. They could even do simple skin grafts, but **surgery** was usually a last resort. If the patient survived the pain, death usually followed from **infection.** Knowledge of **anatomy** was limited because the Church usually opposed **dissection.**

Many medieval treatments are accepted in modern science, but many others had non-scientific roots, such as **astrology.** Doctors were also powerless against **epidemics** of infectious disease, such as influenza and smallpox. Between 1347 and 1351 the Black Death – bubonic plague – killed about a third of the population of Europe.

Doctors were powerless to treat victims during London's last plague epidemic, in 1665, which killed at least 80,000 people.

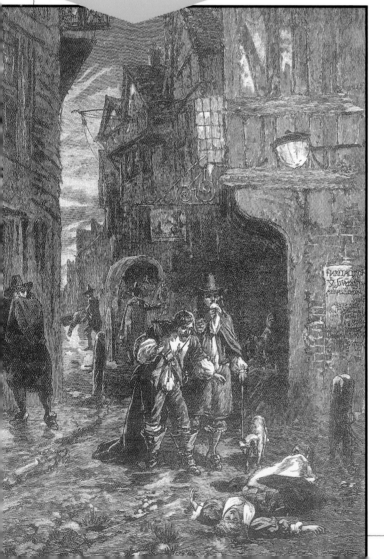

Pioneers of progress

Medical theory and practice improved greatly after 1500, thanks to adventurous new thinkers.

- The German Paracelsus (1493–1541) publicly burned Galen's books and taught that diseases were caused by factors outside the patient, rather than by an 'imbalance' within. He also stressed that doses of medicine should be carefully measured, and was the first to understand that poisons, such as arsenic or mercury, can heal if used in small amounts.
- The Belgian Vesalius (1514–64) revolutionized the study of anatomy with an accurate textbook based on careful – though illegal – dissections.
- Englishman William Harvey (1578–1657) proved that the heart pumped blood round the body, rather than ebbing and flowing like a tide, as Galen had taught.
- Dutchman Antoni van Leeuwenhoek (1632–1723) made a microscope that could give magnified images up to 300 times the size of the object. He was the first to use it to observe blood cells and **bacteria,** and to examine the structure of a human hair and the anatomy of insects. The microscope showed that nature was teeming with **microorganisms** far too small to be seen by the naked eye alone.

Paracelsus burnt the books written by the ancient Greek doctor Galen. They were still being used to teach medicine in 17th-century Europe.

Defeating smallpox

Smallpox is caused by a **virus,** a **microorganism** that spreads in droplets of moisture from an infected person's nose or mouth. Aches and high fever are followed by a rash of pimples that fill with pus, form scabs and leave scars. Four out of five sufferers survive, though they may be scarred and sometimes blinded. For centuries smallpox was a global curse until a new step forward – inoculation – began its complete elimination.

In 1717 Lady Mary Wortley Montagu described what she saw in Turkey:

The smallpox … is here entirely harmless by the invention of engrafting, which is the term they give it … old women … perform the operation every autumn … the old woman comes with a nutshell full of the matter of the best sort of smallpox … She immediately rips open … and puts into the vein as much matter as can lie upon the head of her needle.

Edward Jenner's achievements are commemorated in this plaque beneath his statue in Kensington Gardens in London.

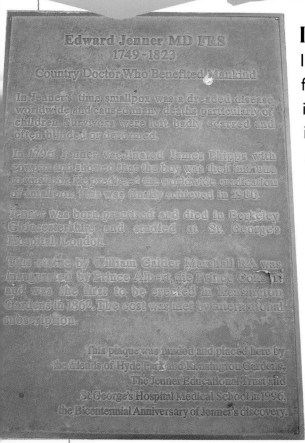

Edward Jenner MD FRS
1749 - 1823
Country Doctor Who Benefited Mankind

In Jenner's time, smallpox was a dreaded disease worldwide and caused many deaths particularly of children. Survivors were left badly scarred and often blinded or deformed.

In 1796 Jenner vaccinated James Phipps with cowpox and showed that the boy was then immune to smallpox. He predicted the worldwide eradication of smallpox. This was finally achieved in 1980.

Jenner was born, practised and died in Berkeley Gloucestershire and studied at St. George's Hospital London.

This statue by William Calder Marshall RA was inaugurated by Prince Albert the Prince Consort and was the first to be erected in Kensington Gardens in 1862. The cost was met by international subscription.

This plaque was funded and placed here by the friends of Hyde Park and Kensington Gardens, The Jenner Educational Trust and St. George's Hospital Medical School in 1996, the Bicentennial Anniversary of Jenner's discovery.

Inoculation

Inoculation means giving a person a weakened form of a disease so that their system produces its own **antibodies** to fight the **infection** and **immunize** them from it in future. Inoculation against smallpox was probably known in ancient India and China.

Inoculation, often using hawthorns instead of needles, was widely practised in 18th-century England, after an experiment on six condemned criminals proved it was safe. Mass inoculations were performed on people judged especially at risk because they were crowded together in prisons, **poorhouses,** army barracks or boarding schools.

Vaccination

Edward Jenner (1749–1823), a country doctor from Berkeley, Gloucestershire, improved on inoculation by developing vaccination – using a **vaccine** (from the Latin vacca, a cow). Jenner was told by local people that milk-maids, who often caught cowpox from the cows they milked, never caught smallpox. In 1796 he vaccinated 8-year-old James Phipps with cowpox scraped from the infected hand of milkmaid Sarah Nelmes. Six weeks later Jenner inoculated James with full-blown smallpox, which failed to develop. James had been successfully immunized.

Jenner published a report of his experiment in 1798. It was translated into seven languages, and vaccination was soon being used to fight a smallpox **epidemic** in far-away Kentucky, USA. Parliament gave Jenner £10,000 and Napoleon ordered a medal to be struck in his honour.

Vaccination was a real breakthrough in medicine but it was based on **folklore** and experience, not science. A century passed before scientists understood what a virus was. In 1966 smallpox was still found in 33 countries, causing up to 15 million cases annually and killing 2 million. By 1980 the World Health Organization was able to announce that it had been completely wiped out.

In 1802, the British Anti-Vaccination Society asked cartoonist James Gillray to forecast the effects of the new treatment. His cartoon shows people who have been vaccinated turning into cows.

Science strengthens medicine

Nineteenth-century scientists working in laboratories made many discoveries that were helpful to doctors. Better communications helped researchers in different countries to cooperate and learn from each other, making science an international concern.

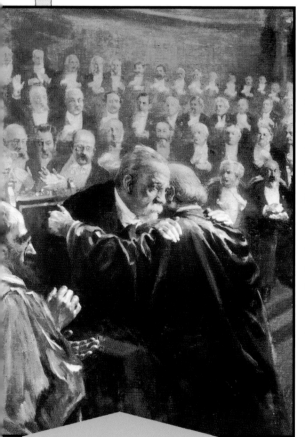

Lister embraces Pasteur at the tribute to Pasteur and his work, held at the Sorbonne Paris, to celebrate the French scientist's 70th birthday.

Pasteur

Frenchman Louis Pasteur (1822–95) was a chemist, not a doctor, but his discoveries changed medicine for ever. Pasteur studied fermentation – the chemical process by which **bacteria**, **moulds** or **yeasts** break down **organic** materials into simpler substances. Fermentation processes are essential in making cheese, wine and beer, but can be harmful. Pasteur discovered that controlled heating kills harmful **microbes.** This process is called *pasteurization*.

Pasteur's most important discovery was that **germs** cause diseases. Many doctors were, however, slow to accept Pasteur's breakthrough, which became known as the 'germ theory' of disease. Building on Jenner's work, Pasteur systematically developed **vaccines** against killer diseases such as anthrax and rabies.

Koch

German doctor Robert Koch (1843–1910), identified the **bacilli** that cause anthrax, tuberculosis and cholera. He also experimented with dyes to stain **microorganisms** so they could be identified more easily.

Semmelweis

Hungarian Ignaz Semmelweis (1818–65) believed that hospital doctors themselves spread **infection.** For example, **puerperal fever** killed twelve out of every hundred mothers who went into hospital to give birth. Semmelweis insisted that washing their hands and instruments thoroughly in a **disinfectant** after examining each patient would prevent doctors from passing infection from one patient to another. At the time, Pasteur's germ theory was not generally known. Other doctors ignored Semmelweis because, although he was correct in accusing them of spreading infection, he could not show how it happened.

Pasteur's follower transforms surgery

Englishman Joseph Lister (1827–1912) quickly accepted Pasteur's germ theory. He thought it explained why almost half of all patients developed fatal infections after **surgery**. In 1867 Lister began soaking his surgical instruments and dressings in carbolic acid, a powerful disinfectant. This procedure, known as '**antiseptic** surgery', cut the number of deaths from infection after operations dramatically. Doctors became more confident about trying more difficult operations on the stomach, throat and head, which would previously have produced fatal infections.

Lister, Pasteur and Koch are honoured on the front of the London School of Hygiene and Tropical Medicine.

A life in science

The discoveries of Pasteur and Lister resulted from patient experiment and methodical tests. In contrast, Alexander Fleming (1881–1955) discovered penicillin by sheer chance, just as chance had made him a researcher in the first place. Born a farmer's son in Ayrshire, Scotland, Fleming grew up keenly interested in plants and wildlife. At 14 he went to London to live with his doctor half-brother, Tom, and learn book-keeping. At 16 Fleming began work as a clerk with the America Line shipping company. At 18 he joined the London Scottish Rifle Volunteers, meeting other young Scots who were living in London and himself becoming a very good shot!

Prize-winning study...

In 1901 an uncle of Fleming's died, leaving him £250 – as much as a skilled workman might earn in a whole year. Suddenly he could afford to train as a doctor, like his brother Tom. He went to St Mary's Hospital, Paddington, which was London's newest teaching hospital. Fleming was a prize-winning student, with time to spare for amateur dramatics and rifle-shooting. When he qualified as a doctor in 1906, John Freeman, a researcher who wanted to keep Fleming on the hospital rifle team, suggested he work alongside him under Almwroth Wright.

Alexander Fleming (front row, left of gangway) as a young medical student at St Mary's Hospital, in Paddington, London.

...and research

Fleming was given the job of taking samples of blood and saliva to grow **bacterial cultures** in **Petri dishes.** He tested them to develop **vaccines.** In 1908 Fleming won a University of London Gold Medal and in 1909 qualified as a surgeon, but by then he was committed to research. Fleming gave up the chance of a career in **surgery** to devote himself to science instead.

Research at war

During World War I Fleming served under Almwroth Wright in a French military hospital, trying to reduce the number of deaths from wound **infections.** Fleming showed that even the strong **antiseptics** first used by Semmelweis and Lister failed to get into the deepest wounds and could even block the body's natural way of healing itself.

Sir Almwroth Wright (1861–1947) returned to the army during World War I. This was the first war in which British soldiers were compulsorily vaccinated against typhoid fever.

THE BOSS

Almwroth Wright (1861–1947), the son of an Irish father and Swedish mother, became chief **pathologist** at the Army School of Medicine. He wanted soldiers going overseas to be vaccinated against **typhoid** fever. The army allowed soldiers to volunteer for vaccination but refused to force them. As a result, during the South African war of 1899–1902, thousands more British soldiers died of typhoid than in battle. Wright left the army in protest, went to St Mary's Hospital and built up a research team. During World War I the army finally followed Wright's advice. Once soldiers were all vaccinated, the number of cases of typhoid fell from 10 to 2 per cent, and the proportion of those who died fell from one in seven to almost none.

Dissolving in tears

An untidy desk

After the war Fleming was given a new laboratory at St Mary's, but his desk remained as famously untidy as ever. Other researchers cleared up daily, but Fleming left **culture** dishes lying around until he needed the space for new ones. Although he worked methodically, he knew scientific discoveries can be accidental. Like his hero, Pasteur, Fleming believed 'chance favours the prepared mind', so it paid to watch for anything unusual.

Alexander Fleming at his desk.

A killer cold

One day Fleming was suffering from a heavy cold, and he decided to culture his heavy nasal **mucus.** The culture dish became **contaminated** by **microorganisms,** either from laboratory dust or blown in from outside. Two weeks later, clearing away some dishes, Fleming noticed that the one with the mucus was covered with golden **bacteria** – but not everywhere. Around the nasal mucus itself the area was clear, and elsewhere bacteria had become clear and lifeless. Fleming concluded that something had spread out from the mucus, preventing **germs** from growing around it and killing off distant bacteria that had already grown.

Testing and reporting

To prove that it was not only his own nasal mucus that had the ability to kill bacteria, Fleming tested samples from other people. Then he discovered that human tears, saliva, blood and even pus all had bacteria-killing powers. Fleming had stumbled on the body's own **antiseptic**, which he called lysozyme, from the Greek word *lysis,* meaning 'dissolving'.

Fleming lectured about lysozyme to the Medical Research Club, but he was not a good public speaker, and he failed to convince his audience that lysozyme was important. He still thought it was, though, partly as one of the ways the body naturally fought **infection** and partly because, unlike strong chemical antiseptics, lysozyme killed bacteria without damaging human cells. He later discovered that lysozyme in egg-white was a hundred times stronger than in human tears. Injecting egg-white solution into rabbits made them more resistant to infection. But Fleming was not a sufficiently skilled chemist to make lysozyme powerful enough for humans. This was finally done at Oxford University in 1937. Since then lysozyme has been used as a gentle antiseptic for eye infections, and for preserving foodstuffs against bacterial decay.

Penicillin

Here, look at this...

In September 1928 Fleming was writing a chapter on the staphylococci group of **bacteria** for a new textbook. It is said that one day he picked up a couple of dishes of staphylococci colonies to show a visitor what he was doing. Fleming then looked closely at one, in surprise. It had contained a particularly harmful kind of bacteria, which usually turned yellow. But Fleming saw a mould on the dish and around it a clear, bacteria-free area.

The tower of St Mary's Hospital, Paddington, London, in which Fleming worked.

Testing...

Fleming set out to investigate this bacteria-killing mould methodically. He put some in a separate dish, let it grow then watered it down. Testing this diluted form, he discovered it would still kill bacteria when it was only $1/500$ of its original strength. Fleming eventually identified the mould as one of a well-known group of brush-shaped **microorganisms** called *Penicillium*, from the Latin word for a fine paint-brush. The particular kind that Fleming showed to have bacteria-killing power was *Penicillium notatum*. Fleming decided to call his discovery 'penicillin'.

Fleming's original penicillin culture plate.

...testing

As with lysozyme, Fleming tried to find where else penicillin could be found, testing moulds from decayed food, rags and old boots. The original penicillin was meanwhile tested for harmful side-effects on mice, rabbits and a human volunteer – Fleming's assistant, Stuart Craddock. Fleming was relieved to find none. Unfortunately it proved difficult to keep penicillin active long enough to try it out as a treatment on actual patients. Its bacteria-killing powers faded after a few days, and Fleming was not a sufficiently expert chemist to stabilize it.

Reporting

Fleming took his research into penicillin as far as he could. In the June 1929 issue of the *British Journal of Experimental Pathology* he published an account of it – the first-ever detailed report of an **antibiotic.** Fleming's lecture to the Medical Research Club on penicillin roused as little interest as his earlier talk on lysozyme. For years nothing further was done with penicillin. Fleming himself turned to testing a new family of drugs, sulphonamides, for which great claims were made. His tests showed that they stopped bacteria spreading but could not kill them off, so patients still needed their own bodies' natural defences to cure them. Meanwhile the possibilities of penicillin were all but forgotten.

A breakthrough at Oxford

Brains from abroad

A **Rhodes Scholarship** brought Australian scientist Howard Florey (1898–1968) to research in Oxford in 1922. By 1935 he was a professor. As an editor of the *British Journal of Experimental Pathology*, Florey knew of Fleming's work almost from its beginnings. Jewish chemist Ernst Chain (1906–79) fled to England from Nazi Germany in 1933. Florey invited Chain to Oxford to do further research on just how lysozyme acted chemically to kill **bacteria.**

Penicillin again

As part of the preparation for his research, Chain read Fleming's 1929 article about penicillin and became interested in the problem of making it in batches large enough, pure enough and active for long enough to be used as a treatment. With Florey's encouragement and the brilliant technical assistance of Norman Heatley, an English researcher from Cambridge, Chain finally succeeded where everyone else had failed. In fact it was later shown that the penicillin they produced was still only 2 per cent pure! Fermentation is a complicated process and not easy to control precisely.

Australian scientist, Howard Florey was awarded the Albert Gold Medal, jointly with Alexander Fleming in 1946, for his part in research on penicillin at Oxford.

More testing

With good supplies of penicillin it became possible to mount extensive tests. One involved injecting 50 mice with streptococci bacteria. Half were then injected with penicillin. After sixteen hours, 24 of the 25 that had received penicillin were still alive – all the rest were dead. Further tests confirmed Fleming's findings of ten years previously – that penicillin was both a dramatically powerful bacteria-killer and quite harmless to animals and humans.

Publishing

In August 1940, a year after the outbreak of World War II, Florey, Chain and Heatley published an account of their research – *Penicillin as a Chemotherapeutic Agent* – in *The Lancet*, Britain's leading medical journal. They naturally paid tribute to Fleming's pioneering work but evidently thought he had died, referring to him as 'the late Professor Fleming'. Fleming, who knew nothing of their work until reading the report in *The Lancet*, went immediately to Oxford, announced himself as 'the late Fleming' and asked 'to see what you've been doing with my old penicillin'. But he took no part in the Oxford team's further researches and returned to St Mary's, tending patients wounded in the bombing of London.

Dr Ernst Chain, the biochemist. With Florey's encouragement and Heatley's help, Chain solved the problem of producing batches of penicillin that were sufficiently large and pure for effective treatment.

A problem of production

Human trials

Between February and June 1941 the Oxford team tried penicillin on six desperately ill patients who had no other hope of recovery. Four survived. It seemed penicillin might save thousands of soldiers from dying of infected wounds. But Oxford could only produce it in quantities large enough for laboratory tests or treating individual patients – not whole armies.

The manager of a New York drugstore (chemist) is shown putting up a sign for the new wonder drug, penicillin, in March 1945.

Help in Illinois

Although Britain had survived the threat of invasion in 1940, its situation was still desperate. Servicemen wounded in battle and civilians wounded in bombings could all benefit from penicillin, but British drug companies lacked the funds to develop large-scale production.

America, however, was rich and still at peace. Florey and Heatley travelled there in July 1941. An old friend of Florey's, Charles Thom, from the US Department of Agriculture, put them in touch with the Research Laboratory in Peoria, Illinois. They asked local people to bring them examples of **mouldy** food in case one might yield an even better source of penicillin. One did – a mouldy melon from a Peoria market, which yielded a chemically stable strain of penicillin ideal for medical use. Thanks to this chance discovery right under their noses, the Peoria team was able to produce penicillin eight times stronger than Oxford had.

America joins in

Japan's attack on Pearl Harbor in December 1941 brought America into the war. Giant US drug companies teamed up with the government to mass-produce medicines for the war effort. Top priority, however, was given to drugs and insecticides to protect troops fighting in tropical areas from bites from poisonous insects and **malaria**, which is carried by mosquitoes. Meanwhile, back in Britain, Florey's wife, Ethel, who was a doctor, tested penicillin on some of her cases. These ranged from abscesses and infected wounds, to a baby's spine severely twisted by osteomyelitis, a bone infection.

A US laboratory technician preparing penicillin under sterile conditions, in 1945.

A wonder drug

By September 1942 penicillin had been used to treat 187 different conditions, sometimes given as an injection, sometimes as an ointment, sometimes swallowed as a medicine – but almost always with success. Fleming himself used it to cure a family friend of meningitis, an infection of the brain or spinal cord which can be fatal – another dramatic 'first'. This led Fleming to contact friends in government and a Penicillin Committee was soon established to get British drug companies to begin mass production.

Into battle

Trial by disaster

On 29 November 1942 a fire at Boston's Cocoanut Grove nightclub caused a stampede, killing nearly 500 and injuring about 200. Many suffered terrible burns, which could easily become infected. Dr Keefer, in charge of US penicillin production, ordered supplies to be released to Massachusetts General Hospital in Boston. News leaked out that the Merck drug company in Rahway, New Jersey, had worked round the clock to rush out a batch of 'an unnamed miracle-drug'.

Keefer was encouraged by the Cocoanut Grove cases to begin testing penicillin on wounded soldiers in spring 1943. Provided the penicillin was given in large enough doses, it became clear that even heavily infected wounds could be cleared up. These tests convinced the US Army to push penicillin production as the drug companies' top priority.

A RACE AGAINST DEATH!

The **Faster** this building is completed...the quicker our wounded men get

Penicillin
THE NEW LIFE-SAVING DRUG

Give this job EVERYTHING You've got!

An American poster shows how penicillin caught the imagination of the public.

Tested in action...

The first large supply of penicillin was delivered to Britain in May 1943, and used under Florey's direction in North Africa in June. Experience there showed it was best used as soon as possible after a wound had been sustained, rather than waiting for the casualty to be evacuated to a safe area.

...with dramatic results

Sufficient penicillin was soon available in Britain to treat victims of factory accidents as well as battle casualties. By D-Day on 6 June 1944, when the Allies landed in France, Ethel Florey was in charge of a special penicillin unit treating 3000 casualties from the Normandy landings. During World War 1 over 12 per cent of wounded soldiers treated in front-line hospitals died of **infections.** In contrast, in 1944 the number was almost zero. By 1945 the US was producing enough penicillin to provide 34 million doses a day.

Large-scale production of penicillin at the Speke factory in Liverpool, England in 1954.

A SOLDIER'S THANKS

As a surgeon at Massachusetts General Hospital, Champ Lyons had used penicillin to treat burns cases from the Cocoanut Grove fire. As US Army Major Lyons, treating GIs wounded in Italy, Champ received the following letter from a soldier with a shattered thigh who clearly realized that he owed his life to penicillin as well as the surgeon's skilled care:

You will not remember me, I was just another scared GI patient to you. But I will surely remember you, always. You ... operated on me ... in Naples. ... I shall never forget those penicillin shots (injections), one every four hours ... for what seemed an eternity.

Because the needles had to be large to allow the penicillin to pass into the body, injections were painful – but they worked.

Prize-winners

Sir Alexander

As penicillin came into general use, the public learned what a massive breakthrough it represented in saving lives. Soon it became clear that the people who had made it possible should be honoured by more than just their fellow scientists. A month after the Allied landings in France, King George VI knighted Alexander Fleming as the original discoverer of penicillin and Howard Florey as leader of the Oxford team that had turned it into a usable treatment.

A year later, in 1945, Fleming and Florey, this time with Chain, met another king, in Stockholm, where the Swedish monarch presented them with the Nobel Prize for Medicine.

Alexander Fleming's Nobel Prize medal.

Celebrity

Howard Florey and Ernst Chain had no wish to become celebrities and returned to their research work. In 1960 Florey was elected to the most honoured position in British science, President of the Royal Society, the first Australian to hold the post. Chain directed an international research centre in Rome and was finally knighted in 1969.

It was left to Fleming to become the centre of public attention. His career as a researcher was over and he had time to enjoy his fame. He also valued the chance to speak out for science in general. He was careful not to exaggerate what he had done, paying tribute to Florey's team and modestly saying, 'Nature makes penicillin; I just found it.'

A global hero

Fleming was honoured by Paddington, where he worked, Chelsea, where he lived, and in Ayrshire, where he was born. He was honoured in France and in Spain and by the Pope. In the USA the Kiowa tribe made him an honorary chief. In dozens of towns and cities, streets and squares were named after him. Fleming died in 1955 and was buried in St Paul's Cathedral, beside Britain's greatest heroes.

A stained-glass window honouring Fleming in St James's, Sussex Gardens, a few minutes' walk from St Mary's Hospital, London, where he worked.

THE NOBEL PRIZE

Alfred Nobel (1833–96), the Swedish inventor of dynamite, left a fortune to fund prizes for outstanding achievements in chemistry, physics, medicine, literature and peace. Prizes were first awarded in 1901. Prize-winners for medicine include Sir Ronald Ross, who discovered how to fight **malaria,** and Sir Frederick Banting, Canadian discoverer of insulin, which is used to treat diabetes.

Battling on

Swallow this

After 1945 there was time and money to develop better types of penicillin. One variety, penicillin V, proved chemically stable when mixed with the natural acid in the patient's stomach. It could therefore be swallowed rather than injected, making it faster, cheaper and less painful to give to patients. Penicillin V became the family doctor's first-choice antibiotic.

Evolution – fast forward

Bacteria have been around for over 3 billion years. As they can reproduce themselves every half-hour or so they evolve much faster than human beings. It was not surprising then that some bacteria developed resistance to penicillin, as Florey noticed as early as 1940. By 1946 London hospitals recorded that 15 per cent of **infections** from the bacteria *Staphylococcus aureus* were resistant to penicillin G, the standard form at the time. By 1947 the figure was 40 per cent, and by 1948 it was 60 per cent. Researchers raced to develop new penicillins to combat resistant bacteria.

Penicillium notatum, Fleming's original source of penicillin, as seen magnified many times through a microscope.

Another step forward

Penicillin did not work against **typhoid** or **salmonella**, and some patients were fatally allergic to it. In 1945 in Sardinia, researcher Giuseppe Brotzu identified a **mould** growing on sewage that could kill typhoid bacilli. In 1961 Florey's team produced cephalosporin – suitable for patients allergic to penicillin and effective against throat infections, typhoid, **pneumonia** and **diphtheria.**

The white plague

The success of penicillin in showing that a mould could produce a useful antibiotic encouraged researchers to test other moulds, in the search for substances that would kill **microbes** unaffected by penicillin.

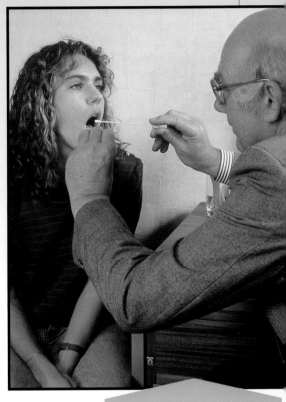

Ordinary soil proved to be a profitable source of moulds. One yielded a cure for tuberculosis (TB) – the white plague – which has probably caused more premature deaths than any other disease in history. One third of the world's population carries the **bacillus** that causes TB, but they will only develop the disease if they are not healthy enough to fight off infection. It kills 3 million people a year, mostly in overcrowded cities in poor countries.

Some patients seem to think that doctors can produce a wonder drug to cure any illness.

French researchers Calmette and Guérin produced a **vaccine** in 1924. In 1943 American Dr Selman A. Waksman, an expert on soil **microorganisms**, discovered streptomycin – the first drug effective against TB. Waksman won the 1952 Nobel Prize for Medicine for this discovery. As streptomycin can sometimes cause dizziness, deafness and kidney damage, it has since been replaced by other drugs. Now, TB is once again on the increase, so the search for better treatments continues.

And next?

Too much of a good thing?

Antibiotics such as penicillin and streptomycin revolutionized the treatment of wounds and disease, saving millions of lives and speeding the process of recovery from – in the case of tuberculosis at least – over a year in hospital to a matter of weeks as an out-patient. By the 1950s, traditional childhood killers such as whooping cough, **diphtheria** and measles, which had caused half of all the deaths in children under 5 in the 1930s, ceased to menace babies and toddlers.

Looking back, it now seems clear that these dramatic successes led to an understandable tendency to over-use the new 'wonder-drugs'. In countries such as the USA and Greece, where they were freely available without having to be prescribed by a doctor, people bought them even for colds, which are caused by a **virus**, against which antibiotics are useless.

Another problem was that patients would stop taking antibiotics as soon as they felt better, rather than finishing the course prescribed. This meant that the **bacteria** in their infected body were not all killed. Surviving bacteria could pass on acquired resistances to other bacteria where they were reproduced in the gut.

It is throught that antibiotics fed to chickens led to resistant bacteria entering the human food chain.

Endless journey

Over-use of antibiotics has provoked bacteria into evolving resistance more quickly than they might otherwise have done. At the same time – since the 1940s – increased international travel, especially by air, has created a sort of global cocktail of bacteria. For

example, HIV, which is associated with AIDS, is still imperfectly understood. One theory is that it originated as a virus **infection** among monkeys in Africa many years – possibly even centuries – ago, just as tuberculosis developed thousands of years ago among cows and was passed on to humans when they drank their milk.

Alexander Fleming in 1955 examining a mould culture in a **Petri dish** in his laboratory at the Wright Fleming Institute in London. Modern research is essentially a team effort.

Air travel hugely speeds up the possible spread of diseases. It took over two years for the Black Death (bubonic plague) to spread from China to Europe. Nowadays a traveller could carry an infection from Hong Kong to London in less than half a day.

Bacteria that cause diseases and the drugs produced to kill them are engaged in a never-ending tussle. The world's major drug companies spend huge amounts of money developing new treatments which, when successful, can yield immense profits. Fleming's discovery of penicillin – made single-handedly and without the backing of a wealthy corporation – was the first vital step that set medical research on a new journey, which still has no end in sight.

Time-line

1717	Lady Montagu observes inoculation in Turkey
1796	Edward Jenner experiments successfully with vaccination against smallpox
1822	Birth of Louis Pasteur
1867	Joseph Lister pioneers the use of antiseptics in surgery
1881	Birth of Alexander Fleming
1888	Pasteur Institute for Research founded in Paris
1898	Birth of Australian Howard Florey
1901	First Nobel Prizes awarded
1914–18	World War I
1922	Fleming discovers lysozyme
1924	Calmette and Guérin develop an anti-tuberculosis vaccine
1928	Fleming discovers penicillin
1935	Florey invites Chain to join his research team in Oxford
1939–45	World War II
1940	Florey, Chain and Heatley publish the results of their laboratory tests on penicillin
1941	United States joins the Allies against Germany and Japan
	Penicillin first used on human patients
1942	Fleming uses penicillin to cure a case of meningitis
1943	Selman Waksman discovers streptomycin
1944	6 June D-day – Allies invade Normandy to begin the liberation of France
	Florey and Fleming are knighted
1945	Fleming, Florey and Chain share Nobel Prize for Medicine
1952	Selman Waksman wins Nobel Prize for Medicine
1955	Death of Sir Alexander Fleming
1960	Florey is elected President of the Royal Society
1961	Florey's team isolate cephalosporin
1980	World Health Organization announces that smallpox has been wiped out world-wide
1987	Azidothymidine (AZT) introduced to combat AIDS
1993	WHO declares a global emergency over re-emergence of TB – 3 million deaths per year
1994	French scientists manufacture Taxol, an anti-cancer drug, from yew-tree needles

lossary

anatomy	study of the structure of the body
antibiotic	substance that kills bacteria, especially those that cause illness
antibodies	natural defence substances produced by the body
antiseptics	chemicals that kill bacteria, especially those that cause disease or rotting
astrology	belief that events can be foretold by the movements of stars and planets
bacillus	bacteria shaped like a rod, such as staphylococci
bacteria	tiny one-celled life-forms visible only through a microscope: some are harmless, others cause rotting or disease
contaminate	mix in something that makes a substance less pure
cultures	bacteria grown experimentally for study
diphtheria	highly infectious disease of the throat, often fatal in children
disinfectant	chemical that kills bacteria that cause infections
dislocation	displaced bone
dissection	cutting up dead bodies to study them
epidemic	widespread outbreak of disease
folklore	popular or traditional beliefs, often based on experience
fracture	break in a bone
germs	popular name for microorganisms that cause disease
immunize	protect against a disease by giving a very mild form of it
infection	disease spread by breathing in or swallowing germs
malaria	infectious disease spread by mosquitoes; sufferers are severely weakened by alternate chills and bouts of fever
microbe/ microorganism	any organism, such as bacteria, viruses, moulds or yeasts, too small to be seen without a microscope
mould	fungus that develops on organic materials (food, leather, cloth)
mucus	slimy substance which protects sensitive skin inside the nose, for example
organic	something that is living or has lived
pathologist	expert on the causes of disease and death
Petri dish	shallow glass container used in a laboratory to grow cultures
pneumonia	infection that causes the lungs to fill with liquid, causing death when the patient can no longer breathe
poorhouse	hostel where people too poor to keep themselves were fed and sheltered, often in harsh conditions
puerperal fever	form of blood poisoning caused by infection caught during childbirth
Rhodes Scholarship	award funded by money given by diamond millionaire Cecil Rhodes (1853–1902) to enable outstanding students from the USA and Commonwealth countries to study at Oxford University
salmonella	type of bacteria, many varieties of which cause food-poisoning
surgery	cutting into the body to repair damage or remove infection
typhoid	highly infectious and often fatal fever caused by a bacillus
vaccine	substance used to immunize against a particular disease
virus	microorganism that can only reproduce within the cells of something living
yeast	single-celled form of fungus

Index

Titles in the *Turning Points* series include:

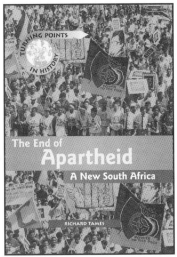

Hardback   0 431 06919 0

Hardback   0 431 06918 2

Hardback   0 431 06920 4

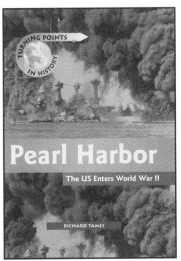

Hardback   0 431 06917 4

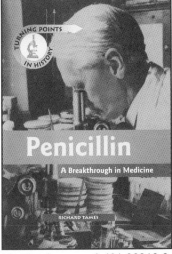

Hardback   0 431 06916 6

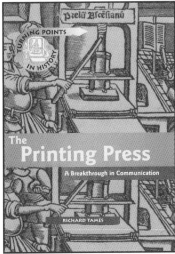

Hardback   0 431 06921 2

Find out about the other titles in this series on our website www.heinemann.co.uk/library